W9-AHT-779

Torringford School LMC
800 Charles Street
Torrington, CT 06790
(860)489-2300

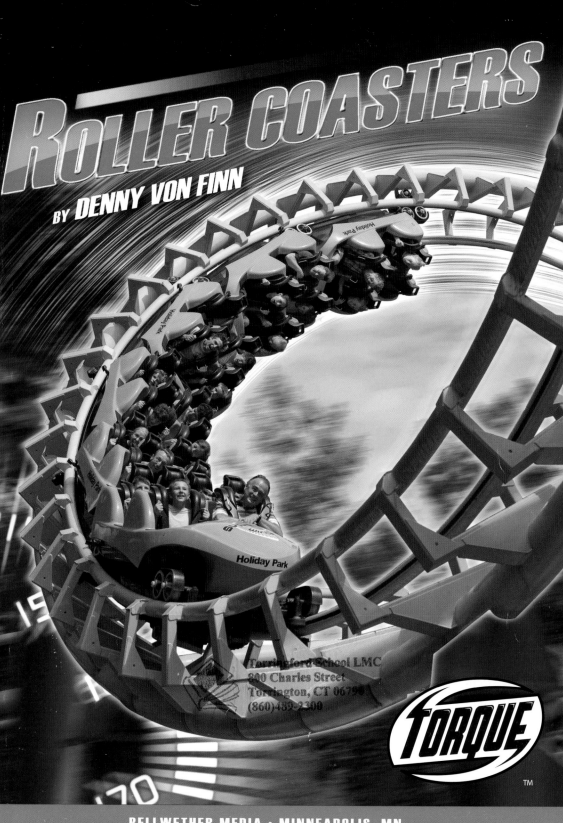

ROLLER COASTERS

BY DENNY VON FINN

TORQUE™

BELLWETHER MEDIA • MINNEAPOLIS, MN

Are you ready to take it to the extreme? Torque books thrust you into the action-packed world of sports, vehicles, and adventure. These books may include dirt, smoke, fire, and dangerous stunts. **WARNING:** read at your own risk.

This edition first published in 2010 by Bellwether Media, Inc.

No part of this publication may be reproduced in whole or in part without written permission of the publisher. For information regarding permission, write to Bellwether Media, Inc., Attention: Permissions Department, 5357 Penn Avenue South, Minneapolis, MN 55419.

Library of Congress Cataloging-in-Publication Data

Von Finn, Denny.
 Roller coasters / by Denny Von Finn.
    p. cm. -- (Torque books. The world's fastest)
 Includes bibliographical references and index.
 Summary: "Amazing photography accompanies engaging information about roller coasters. The combination of high-interest subject matter and light text is intended for students in grades 3 through 7"--Provided by publisher.
 ISBN 978-1-60014-337-3 (hardcover : alk. paper)
 1. Roller coasters--Juvenile literature. I. Title.
 GV1860.R64V66 2010
 791.06'8--dc22   2009037942

Text copyright © 2010 by Bellwether Media, Inc.
Printed in the United States of America, North Mankato, MN.

010110   1149

CONTENTS

What Are Roller Coasters?

Roller coasters are rides that provide great speed and excitement. They also have steep hills. Today's tallest roller coasters rise more than 400 feet (122 meters) above the ground. The *Kingda Ka* roller coaster is 456 feet (139 meters) tall. It can **accelerate** from 0 to 128 miles (0 to 206 kilometers) per hour in 3.5 seconds!

Kingda Ka

Roller coasters have features similar to a railroad. A roller coaster has a **train** of cars that carries riders on a track. The train speeds up and down the track. A few coasters even have tracks that go straight up and down. Many of today's coasters **invert** riders.

Fast Fact

Riders in suspended and inverted coasters hang underneath the rails. Riders even stand up or lie down on some coasters!

The first ride with wheels that locked to tracks opened in France in 1817. Similar rides soon became popular. L. M. Thompson opened a "switch-back railway" in 1884. Cars carried riders 600 feet (183 meters) down a track. A new group of riders rode the cars back on a second track. Thompson called this a "Roller Coasting Structure."

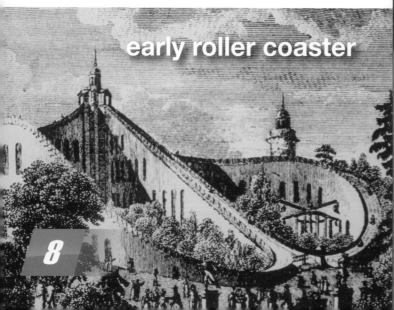

early roller coaster

The Steel Dragon 2000

Fast Fact

The *Steel Dragon 2000* in Japan is the world's longest roller coaster. It is 8,133 feet (2,479 meters) long. A ride lasts 4 minutes.

Roller Coaster Technology

Early roller coasters were made of wood. Steel tracks were attached to the top of wood supports. These coasters are called **woodies**.

Disneyland introduced the first steel roller coaster in 1959. Steel can be bent in any direction. This lets designers make the twisting coasters that are popular today. The first **corkscrew** roller coaster opened in 1975 at Knott's Berry Farm in California.

A roller coaster has three kinds of wheels.
Running wheels roll on top of the track.
Under-friction wheels roll beneath the track.
Both kinds of wheels work together. They help
the train grab the track. **Side-friction wheels** roll
along the outside of the track. They give the train a
smooth ride.

running wheel

side-friction wheel

under-friction wheel

ring° racer

Fast Fact

The *ring°racer* coaster in Germany can accelerate to 135 miles (217 kilometers) per hour in 2.5 seconds. That's twice as quick as a Formula 1 race car!

Classic roller coasters begin with a **lift hill**. A chain under the track pulls the train up the lift hill. Then **gravity** takes over. Modern coasters have **launch mechanisms**. These mechanisms create more speed than gravity can create. Some launch mechanisms use electric motors. Others use pressurized air or liquid to launch the cars.

Roller coasters cause riders to experience a high **g-force**. The g-force gives riders a funny feeling in their stomachs. Some coaster designers ask astronauts and jet pilots about g-forces. They want to be sure g-forces on their coasters are safe for riders.

The Future of Roller Coasters

Roller coasters of the future will have even more thrills and higher speeds. Many coaster fans still love woodies. Amusement parks around the world continue to build faster and longer wooden coasters.

Son of Beast is one of the largest, fastest woodies in the world. It is 7,032 feet (2,143 meters) long and has a top speed of 78 miles (126 kilometers) per hour!

Computers help designers create more extreme coasters. Roller coasters more than 500 feet (152 meters) tall are now possible. That's nearly as tall as a 50-story building!

Computers will also help designers create faster coasters. Perhaps coaster riders will one day accelerate as quickly as jet airplanes!

GLOSSARY

accelerate—to increase speed

corkscrew—a part of a roller coaster that inverts riders in a series of rolls

g-force—the force that acceleration puts on a coaster rider

gravity—the force that pulls objects toward Earth

invert—to turn a rider upside down

launch mechanisms—devices that accelerate a train at the beginning of a run

lift hill—the first hill at the beginning of a roller coaster run

running wheels—car wheels that run on top of the track

side-friction wheels—car wheels that run on the outside of the track to smooth the ride

train—two or more roller coaster cars hooked together

under-friction wheels—car wheels that run beneath the track

woodies—roller coasters with tracks supported by wooden frames

TO LEARN MORE

AT THE LIBRARY

Frazee, Marla. *Roller Coaster*. San Diego, Calif.: Harcourt, 2003.

Goldish, Meish. *Heart-Stopping Roller Coasters*. New York, N.Y.: Bearport Publishing, 2010.

Mason, Paul. *Roller Coaster! Motion and Acceleration*. Chicago, Ill.: Heinemann Library, 2007.

ON THE WEB

Learning more about roller coasters is as easy as 1, 2, 3.

1. Go to www.factsurfer.com.

2. Enter "roller coasters" into the search box.

3. Click the "Surf" button and you will see a list of related Web sites.

With factsurfer.com, finding more information is just a click away.

The images in this book are reproduced through the courtesy of: J W Alker, front cover, pp. 16-17; AFP / Getty Images, pp. 4, 10; Marcio Silva, p. 5; David Wall / Alamy, p. 6; Chris Fourie, p. 7; Mary Evans Picture Library / Alamy, p. 8 (small); Janma, pp. 8-9; Bob Torrez, p. 11; Chuck Eckert / Alamy, p. 12; JHP Attractions, p. 13; Rommel, p. 14; S&S Worldwide, p. 15; Oliver Gerhard, p. 18; Al Behrman / Associated Press, p. 19; Associated Press, pp. 20, 21.